How to Register a Domain Name

It's Your Business Identity

Book 3 in the Internet Marketing FAST Series

Copyright and Enquiries

Contents

How to Register a Domain Name

It's Your Business Identity

Table of Figures

How to Register a Domain Name

It's Your Business Identity

Register a Domain Name

Your Domain Name is Your Business Address

Figure 1: Your Domain Name

Just as a good street address is important to a bricks and mortar business, a good domain name is important to an online business.

But what makes a good domain name?

Well, first of all, it has to reflect your business. When a prospective visitor sees it, they should be in no doubt as to what your business is about.

In addition, these are the other desirable characteristics:

It should have a dot com extension

The shorter the better, as long as it still makes sense. All the single word domains are long gone, and most of the two-word ones. If you can summarize your story in three words and they're available as a .com domain name, that's great.

For example, if I wanted to create a website that was all about coffee (a very popular subject) and use affiliate links to sell associated product,

How to Register a Domain Name
It's Your Business Identity

including high ticket items like fully automatic coffee machines, here are some domain names I could be investigating:

allcoffeelovers.com

thecoffeebarista.com

thedailygrind.com

coffeeforall.com

You just need a bit of imagination and just keep coming up with variations until you find one that no one else has thought of.

It's Not Your Domain That Ranks

This might seem counter-intuitive, but it's not your website that you will be trying to rank high in Google and the other search engines.

Let me explain.

Your website comprises a number of pages. In WordPress terminology, some of these will be "pages" and some will be "posts".

Broadly speaking, a page contains permanent information and a post is an informative article about a specific thing related to your website.

It's the posts and pages that you will be trying to rank *for a particular keyword*.

Sticking with our coffee example, you might have a page with images and text for 5 top-end espresso coffee machines sold by Amazon, containing your Amazon affiliate link.

How to Register a Domain Name

It's Your Business Identity

You then write a post titled "The 5 Best Espresso Coffee Machines Reviewed" with a detailed review of each one and a recommendation. The post contains a link to your sales page.

What you are trying to achieve is for your post to appear on page 1 when someone does a search on "best espresso coffee machines" or "espresso coffee machines review" or similar.

Do you see the difference? It's not your website itself that you're ranking but a particular post leading to a potential sale.

Gone are the days when people remembered your domain name and typed it in. Everyone finds stuff by searching for a relevant term in Google, Bing or another search engine.

The broader your target market, the less specific your domain name needs to be. As examples, what do the words "Google" or "Bing" or "Yahoo" have to do with searching the internet?

Perhaps even more significantly, what does "Amazon" have to do with becoming the biggest retailer in the world?

You're unlikely to become the next Amazon, so your domain name should reflect your business, but don't stress about it. You can always find something relevant.

Don't buy a domain name on the secondary market. It's an unnecessary expense.

How to Register a Domain Name

It's Your Business Identity

What Are All These TLDs (Top Level domains)?

Figure 2: Top Level Domains

How to Register a Domain Name

It's Your Business Identity

TLDs (Top Level Domains) are what appears to the right of the dot in your domain name.

The name you've chosen, that appears to the left of the dot, is called an SLD (Second Level Domain).

Originally, there were just three TLDs.

.com was for commercial websites like yours.

.org was for non-profit or charitable websites.

.net was for everything else on the internet. Then .info was added for sites designed to inform and educate.

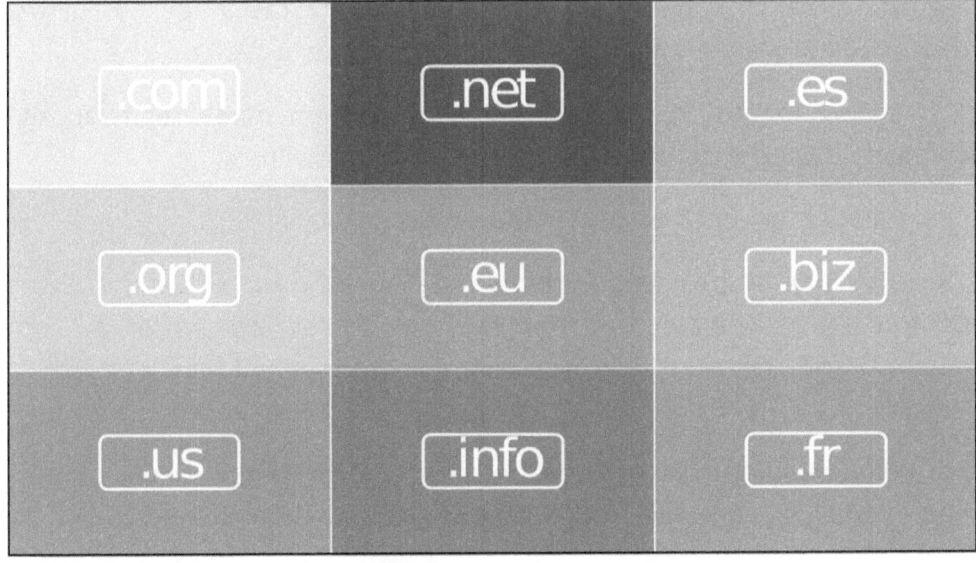

Figure 3: Some TLDs

Since then, there have been a proliferation of TLDs, such as .biz, .pro, .tv and so on, with new ones being constantly added. This has happened partly because of the explosion of websites, to make more possibilities available, but also simply because the more available, the more potential profit there is for the domain name registrars.

However, this has also resulted in the .com version becoming more and more valuable and highly regarded.

The upshot is simply this. Get a .com domain for your website.

How to Register a Domain Name

A domain name registrar is a company that manages the reservation of Internet domain names. The company must be accredited by a generic top-level domain (gTLD) registry or a country code top-level domain (ccTLD) registry. A registrar operates in accordance with the guidelines of the designated domain name registries.

This simply means that to operate as a domain name registrar, the company must be accredited and follow strict guidelines.

There are a number of domain name registrars available.

These include Namecheap, Crazy Domains, Monika, GoDaddy, eNom Central, Crazy Domains and many others. Prices are similar but not identical and different registrars will have various specials at different times.

My recommended registrars are Namecheap for global (.com) domain names and Crazy Domains for Australian (.com.au) domain names.

Using Namecheap

Go to Namecheap using this link.

How to Register a Domain Name

It's Your Business Identity

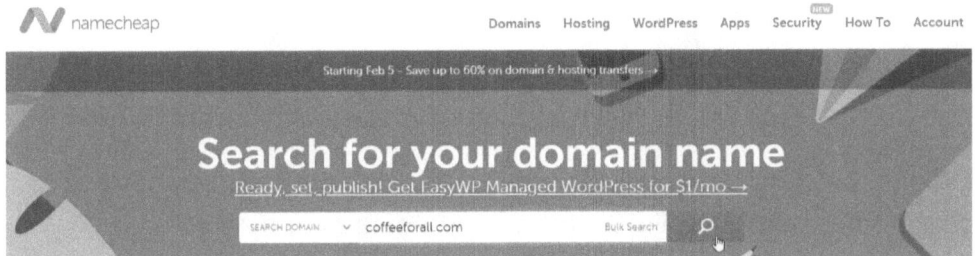

Figure 4: Search for Your Domain Name

Enter the domain you want and press Enter or click on the Search icon.

I've entered one of the coffee-oriented domains we considered earlier.

Namecheap will tell me if coffeeforall.com is available.

Figure 5: Domain Name Not Available

As expected, this particular domain name isn't available.

How to Register a Domain Name

It's Your Business Identity

Namecheap will tell you what other TLDs are available and you can scroll down to see them all. There are hundreds of them.

But we are only interested in the .com, so let's try some other possibilities.

What if we substituted youandme for all? It's a bit long, but not bad and rolls off the tongue easily. So let's try coffeeforyouandme.com.

Figure 6: Successful Domain Name Search

And there we have it, a successful domain name search. We could continue searching from here or we could decide to go with this one by clicking on *add to cart* and paying $8.88 for a year's registration.

Note: coffeeforyouandme.com was available when this book was written. It may not be available now.

Namecheap Domain Name Registrar

You've seen how you can use Namecheap to check out possible domain names until you find one that you're happy with. Then register and purchase for just $8.88.

You can go to Namecheap HERE.

Use Domain Wheel for Inspiration

A useful tool to help you research domain names is https://domainwheel.com/.

How to Register a Domain Name

It's Your Business Identity

Open Domain Wheel in one tab and Namecheap in another.

Enter your seed word into Domain Wheel, check only the .com extension and click *Search Domain*.

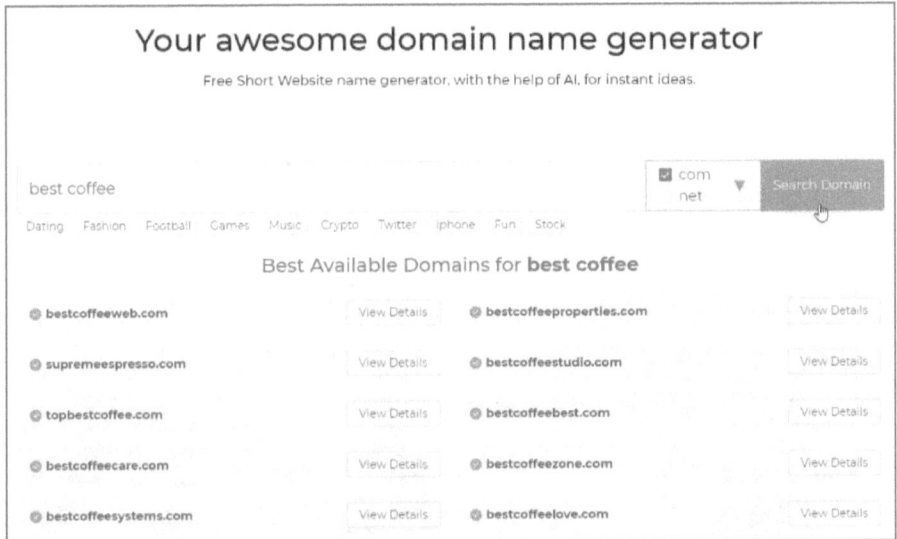

Figure 7: Domain Name Generator

If you don't see a suitable domain name, try a different seed word.

When you find a good name, go to Namecheap and register it.

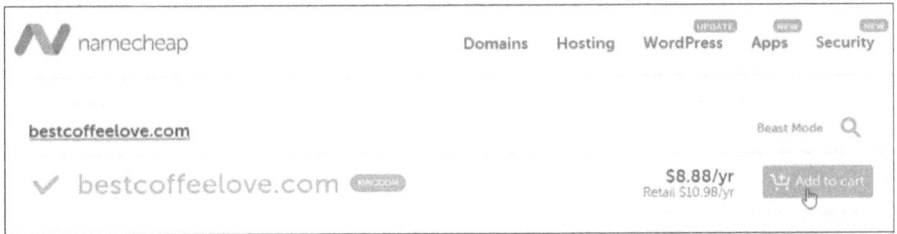

Figure 8: Register the Domain You Found

How to Register a Domain Name

It's Your Business Identity

Transferring a Domain Name

Crazy Domains

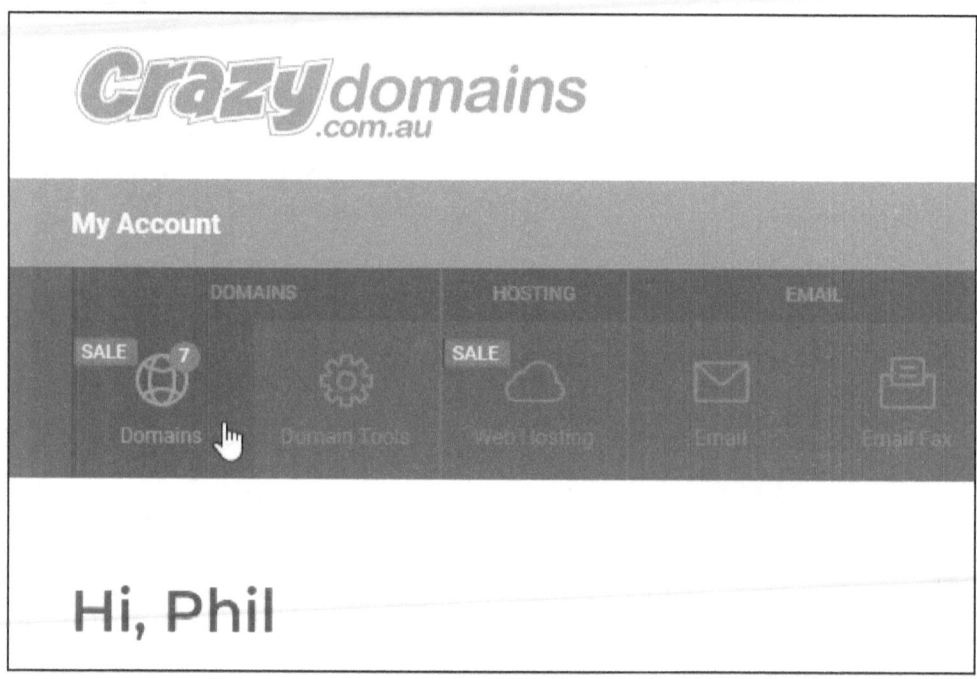

Figure 9: Click on Domains

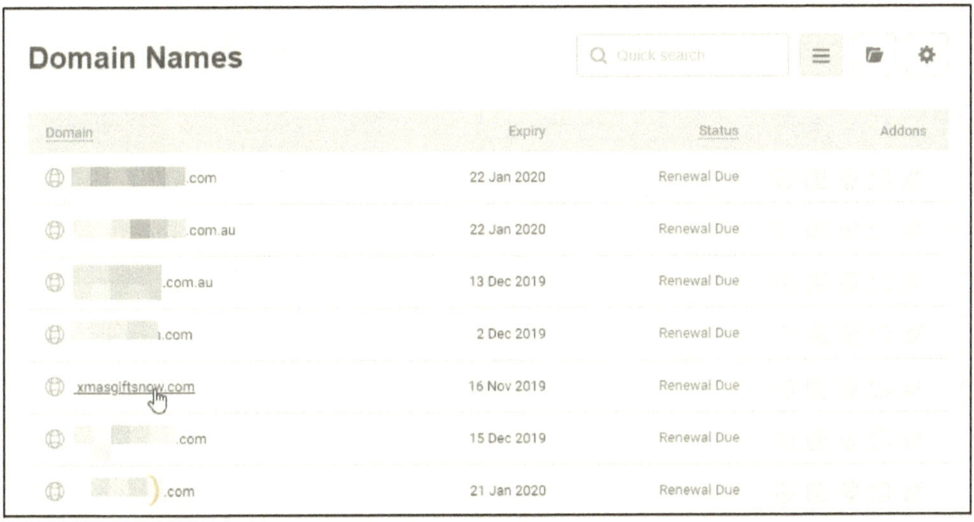

How to Register a Domain Name

It's Your Business Identity

Domain	Expiry	Status	Addons
.com	22 Jan 2020	Renewal Due	
.com.au	22 Jan 2020	Renewal Due	
.com.au	13 Dec 2019	Renewal Due	
.com	2 Dec 2019	Renewal Due	
xmasgiftsnow.com	16 Nov 2019	Renewal Due	
.com	15 Dec 2019	Renewal Due	
) .com	21 Jan 2020	Renewal Due	

Figure 10: Click on the Domain Name to be Transferred

How to Register a Domain Name

It's Your Business Identity

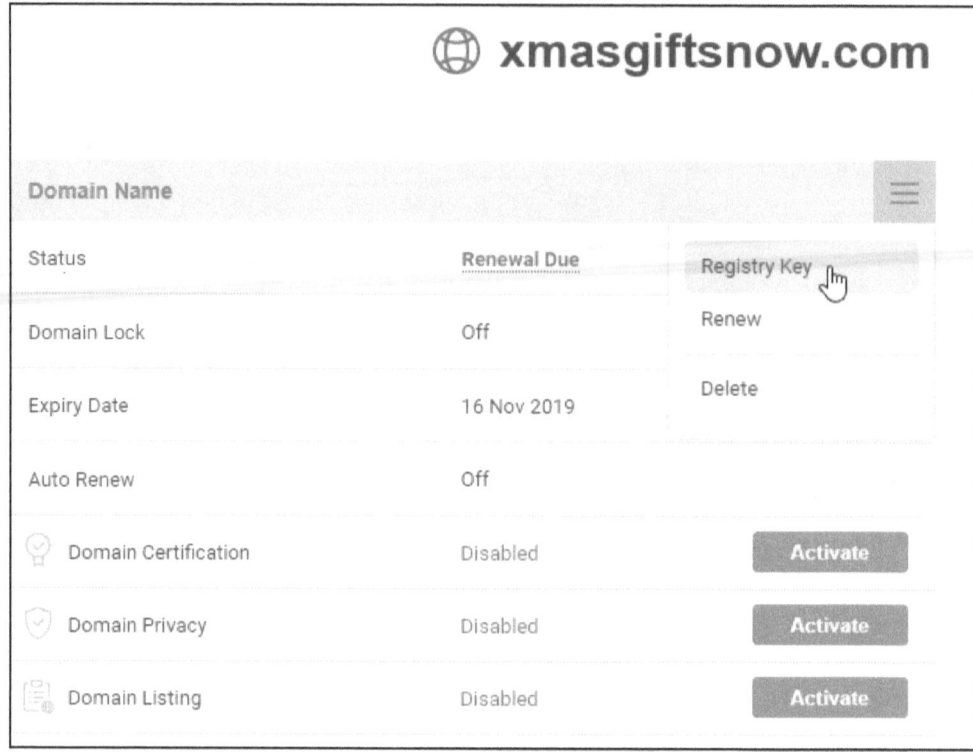

Figure 11: Select Registry Key

How to Register a Domain Name

It's Your Business Identity

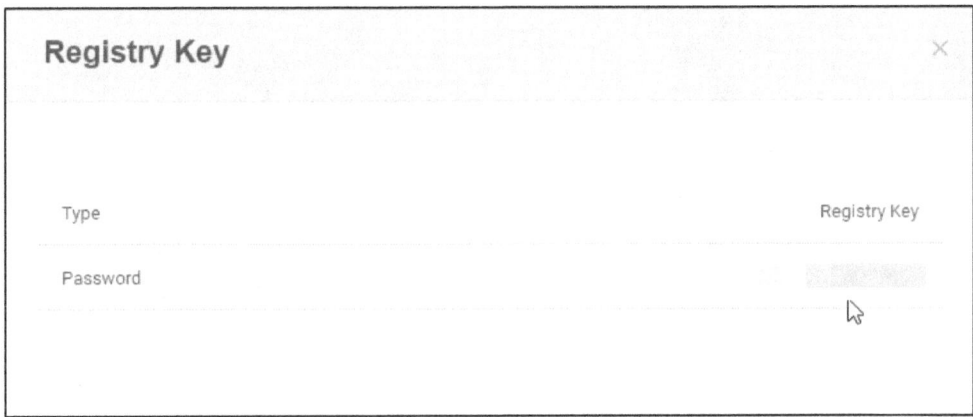

Figure 12: Copy the Registry Key Password

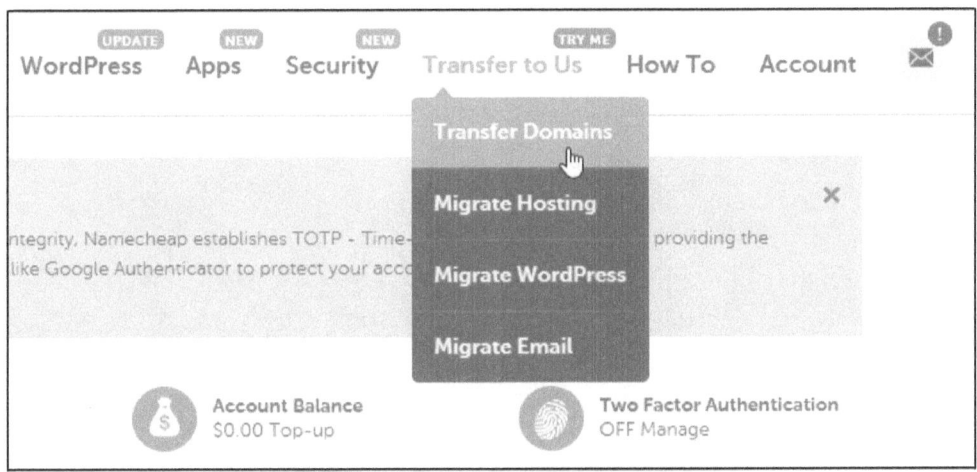

Figure 13: Click on Transfer Domains

How to Register a Domain Name

It's Your Business Identity

Figure 14: Enter the Domain Name and Click Transfer

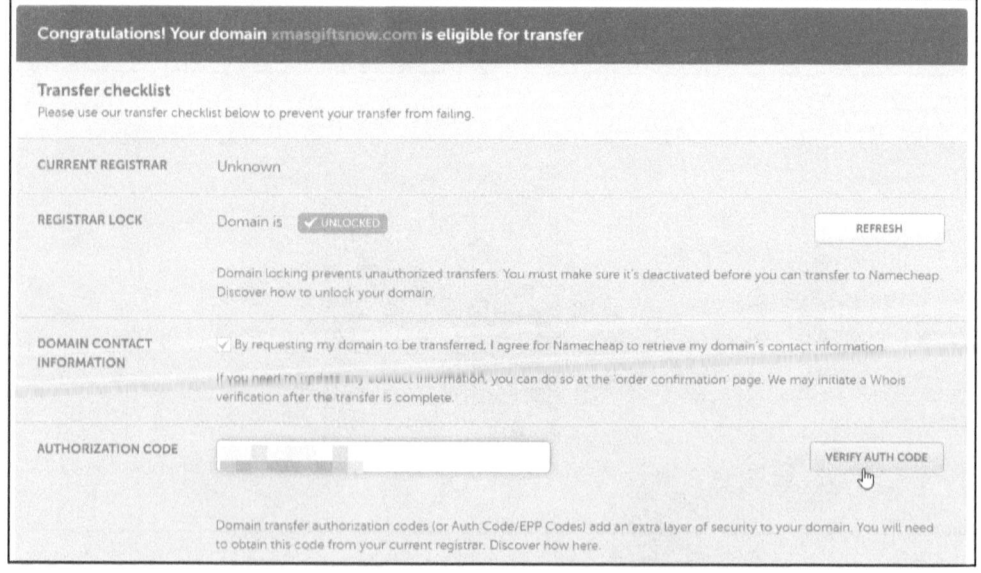

Figure 15: Enter and Verify the Authorization Code

How to Register a Domain Name

It's Your Business Identity

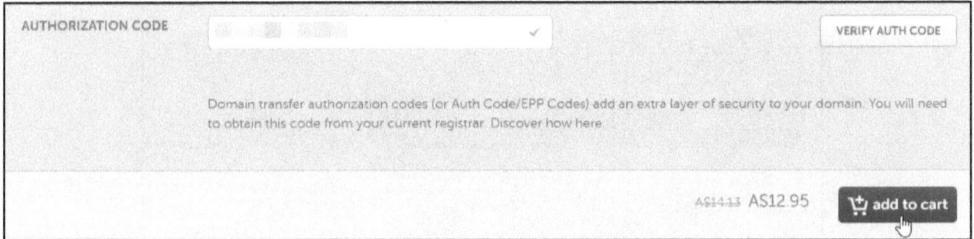

Figure 16: Add to Shopping Cart

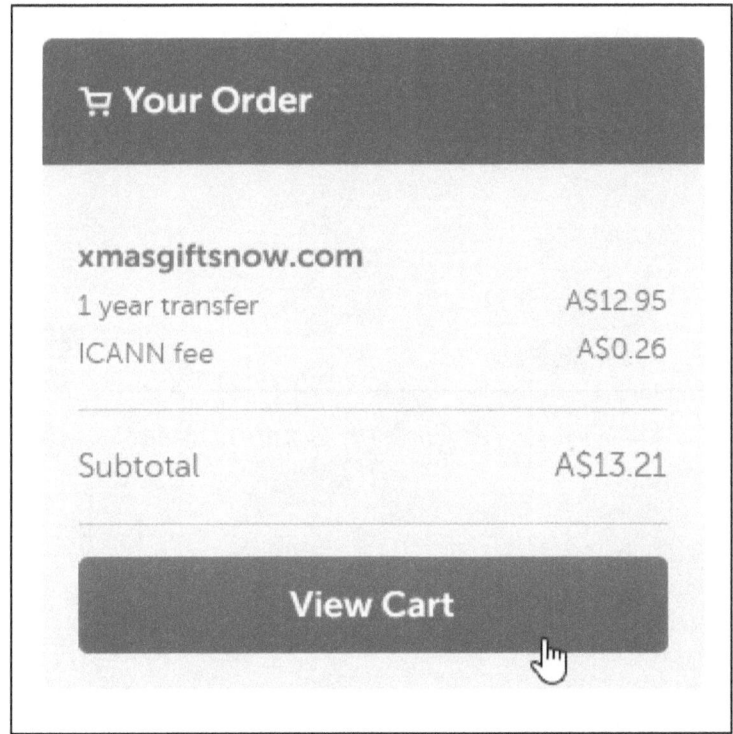

Figure 17: Click on View Cart

How to Register a Domain Name

It's Your Business Identity

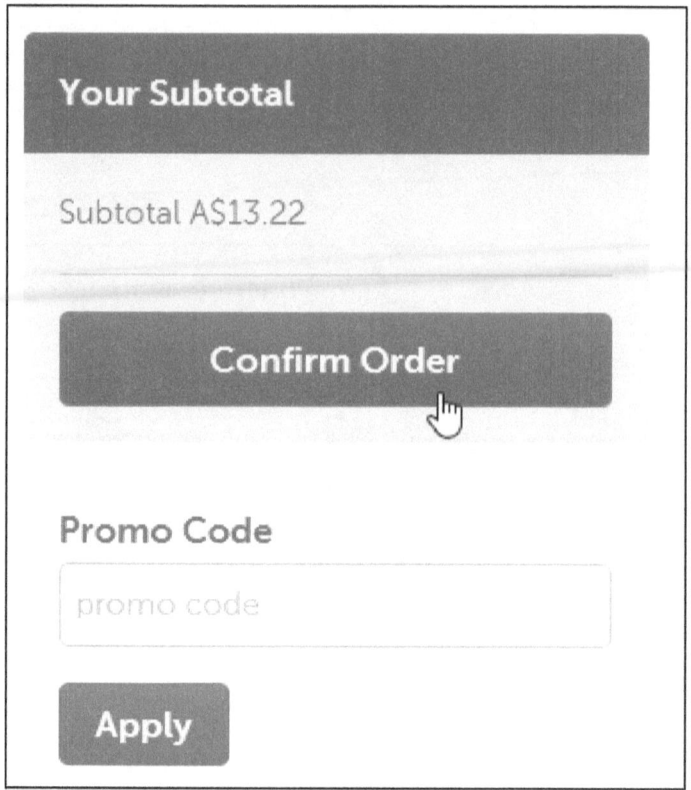

Figure 18: Click on Confirm Order

How to Register a Domain Name

It's Your Business Identity

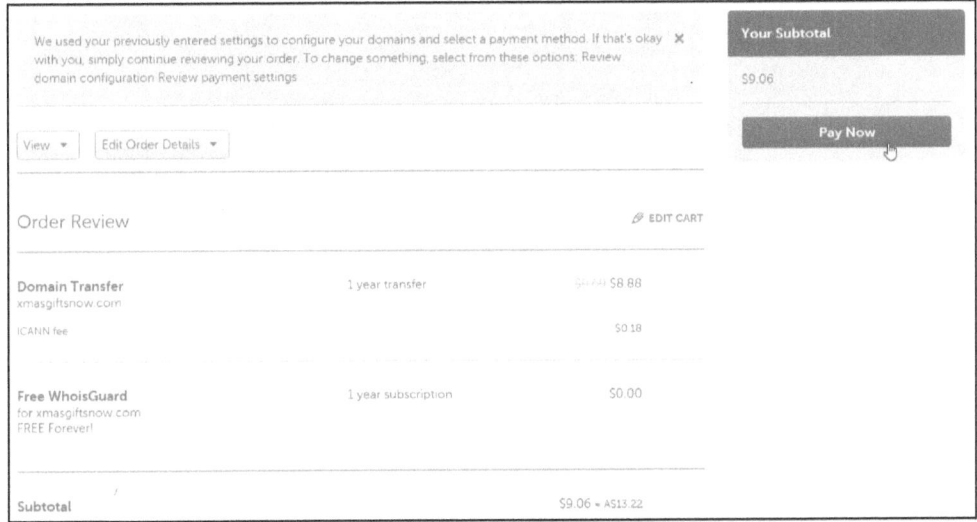

Figure 19: Review Your Order and Click Pay Now

How to Register a Domain Name

It's Your Business Identity

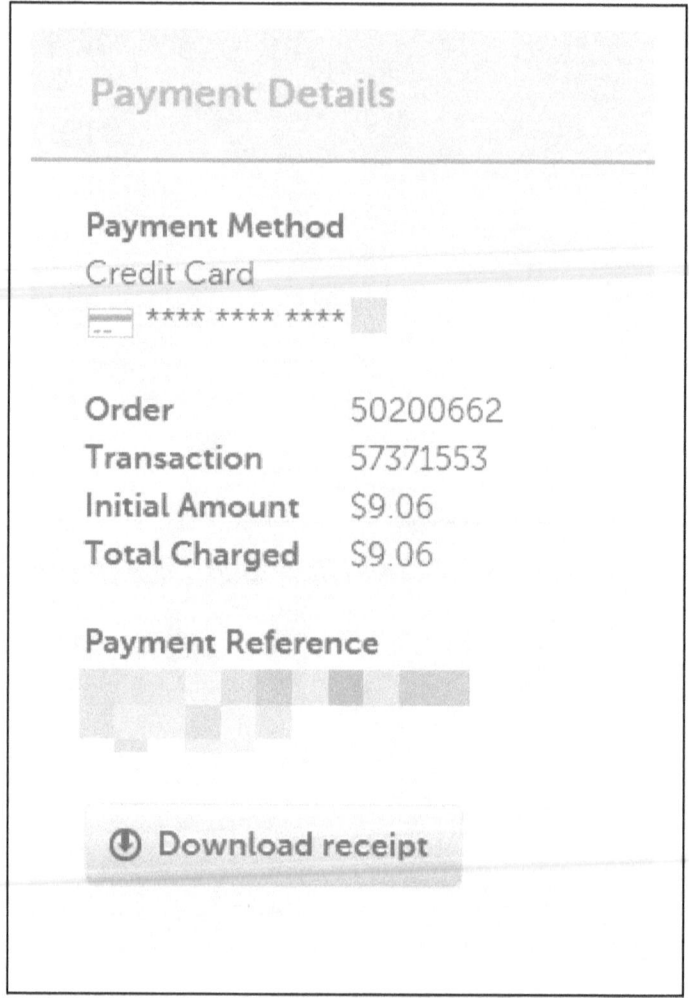

Figure 20: Previously Entered Payment Details

How to Register a Domain Name

It's Your Business Identity

Purchase Summary			
Domain Transfer xmasgiftsnow.com	1 year	~~$9.69~~ **$8.88**	MANAGE
ICANN fee		$0.18	
Free WhoisGuard	1 year	$0.00	MANAGE
Initial Charged		$9.06	
Total Charged		$9.06	

Figure 21: Domain Transfer is Complete

Carry Time Over
Add any remaining time to your 1-year renewal

Zero Downtime
Keep your site running without any downtime

Personal Data Privacy
Get free lifetime WhoisGuard privacy protection

Figure 22: Some Namecheap Benefits

How to Register a Domain Name
It's Your Business Identity

The Rest of the Books

Here are all the books in my Internet Marketing FAST series, all available as Kindle Singles.

Available Now on Amazon

1. The 4 Things You Must Know (to Make Money While You Sleep)
2. How to Select Your Internet Marketing Niche
3. How to Register a Domain Name
4. How to Host Your Website
5. WordPress for the Technically Challenged
6. Building Your Website with Thrive
7. The Thrive User
8. The Thrive Expert

Not Yet Available

9. Become an Affiliate Marketing Ninja
10. Become an E-Commerce Ninja
11. The Deadly Combo of Blog Posts and Landing Pages
12. Google is Your New Best Friend
13. Building Your Mailing List
14. All About Free and Paid Traffic
15. How to Publish Your Book on Amazon
16. The Secret to Making Money with Your Internet Businesses (after You've Done Everything Else)

How to Register a Domain Name

It's Your Business Identity

About the Author

As an 80 year old (in 2024) fitness fanatic and successful internet marketer, Phil Lancaster is a bit of an anomaly.

Through a combination of bad luck and bad business decisions, he found himself broke and alone at 74.

Now, a few years later, he has several internet businesses that combine to bring him a 6-figure income.

It wasn't easy and he got burned a few times on the way, but he reckons that anyone can do it with the right road map.

He wants to help you to get started the way he did, but without making the same mistakes.

Anyone, from student to baby boomer (and older) can make money through the internet.

Phil's IM Fast series of mini-books will get you started. At just $2.99 each, you won't find a better investment.

Unless it's his Affiliate Marketing FAST training course. Register your interest now at https://imfasttraining.com/register-your-interest/.